ESL for Job Success

On-the-Job English

Teacher's Guide

Christy M. Newman

New Readers Press

On-the-Job English
ISBN 1-56420-148-1
Copyright © 2000
New Readers Press
Division of ProLiteracy Worldwide
1320 Jamesville Ave., Syracuse, New York 13210

Printed in the United States of America
9 8 7 6 5 4 3

Director of Acquisitions and Development: Christina Jagger
Developmental Editor: Paula L. Schlusberg
Production Director: Deborah Christiansen
Copy Editor: Judi Lauber
Design: Patricia A. Rapple
Cover Design: Kimbrly Koennecke

Contents

Overview 4

Key Features of *On-the-Job English* 4

Features of Units 1–4 4

Features of the Lessons 5

Using the Lessons 5

Adapting Lessons to Specific Workplace Settings 7

Useful Additions to Lesson Material 7

SCANS Correlations to *On-the-Job English* Lessons 8

Lesson Notes 10

Unit 1 10

Unit 2 17

Unit 3 22

Unit 4 27

Overview

On-the-Job English is designed to teach and re-inforce key functional language skills that high-beginning- to intermediate-level ESL students need to communicate successfully in the American workplace. Its theme-based, integrated-skills approach helps students develop language skills and strategies so they can

- express basic workplace needs
- understand, follow, and give oral and written instructions
- document and discuss work completed
- understand and follow safety guidelines, report safety problems, and respond to warnings on the job
- participate in meetings by expressing and responding to opinions
- follow work schedules
- understand and respond to announcements, job postings, and memos

A premise of On-the-Job English is that adult ESL students already have rich language skills and experiences. Lesson activities are designed to capitalize on those skills and experiences and to elicit students' active participation as they adapt to work in a new culture and country.

The language in On-the-Job English reflects a typical American workplace. Lessons and activities are set in specific workplaces, but they can easily be adapted to fit other work settings.

Key Features of On-the-Job English

Table of Contents, About This Book, and Needs Assessment and Goal Setting

Every component of a student text should provide opportunities for learning. The table of contents is a guide for exploring the book before starting the lessons. Students can use the table of contents to focus on their learning goals and to find the sections of On-the-Job English that address those goals.

About This Book explains concisely the goals of On-the-Job English and what students can expect to accomplish.

By using Needs Assessment and Goal Setting, students can identify and express their needs and goals. Completing Needs Assessment and Goal Setting is a learning activity in itself. It also helps students focus on the skills they need and want to work on.

Developing that self-awareness is a critical function of assessment. Students first identify how they currently use or need to use English in the workplace. Based on that information, students identify personal, practical learning goals. Needs and goals should be reviewed periodically—for example, after every unit—to allow students to evaluate their progress.

Self-Evaluation and Answer Key

At the end of On-the-Job English, students are asked to complete a process-oriented self-evaluation. In this evaluation, they reflect on their progress towards their original goals. Some they will have achieved. Others they may still need work on. Still others they may have discarded. Then, they set new language goals. Finally, they reflect on and write about how they use their new skills at their jobs.

At the back of the student text is an answer key for the short-answer exercises. This allows students to work independently and to correct their work in small groups. It also helps students understand how to respond when they are having trouble with an exercise.

Features of Units 1–4

On-the-Job English is made up of four units, each containing four or five lessons. Unit themes are

- Communicating about a Job
- Following Safety Procedures
- Working with Others
- Using Company Communications

Unit Openers and Unit Reviews

Each unit opens with a page that introduces the theme, which will be developed in each lesson of the unit. A lively illustration helps students focus on the topics covered in the lessons. By discussing the opening text and illustration, you can access students' prior knowledge and experience. For example, the text includes broad questions that introduce the communicative tasks addressed in the lessons. The illustration can elicit relevant vocabulary or experiences.

Each unit closes with a review page that lets students integrate key points from the unit and assess what they have learned.

Features of the Lessons

The lessons in *On-the-Job English* can be taught effectively in any sequence, according to the needs and priorities of the students and the program. Activities encourage students to develop the critical-thinking and problem-solving skills crucial for job success. They also encourage work in groups or teams, which is typical of many workplaces. Students practice language skills in simulated real-life interactions: between co-workers, between workers and supervisors or administrators, and between workers and customers. The language skills covered are suitable to many work settings, so students from different workplaces can easily study together. The activities can be customized to use vocabulary and work tasks of specific jobs. The language skills developed will also transfer easily to many different workplaces.

Each lesson includes

- a list of objectives
- an introductory illustration and Warm-Up activities
- Key Words, presented in visual form
- a conversation or workplace document that presents core functional language
- Tips on applying the skills presented
- comprehension activities, including an exercise to check basic understanding and discussion questions to guide analysis of the communication task

- exercises and activities that utilize and extend language skills presented in the lesson
- Try It Out, a practice activity that simulates natural language in a workplace
- a two-part Wrap-Up (One part analyzes a feature of workplace culture; the other applies the lesson content to students' own work experiences.)

Using the Lessons

This section provides general suggestions for using the main lesson features. For specific suggestions for teaching each lesson, see the Lesson Notes starting on page 10.

Objectives

Reviewing lesson objectives lets students anticipate where a lesson is going and what they will accomplish. This helps them be active players in their own learning.

Warm-Up

The Warm-Up is a two-part activity. First, several questions get students talking about their own experience to prepare for the lesson topic. Then, the illustration provides a visual introduction to the central conversation or reading. Questions about the illustration tap into relevant knowledge and experience. Students can identify items shown, predict who the people shown are, and describe what the people seem to be doing. They can explore visual clues to relationships and emotions. As students move on in the lesson, they can refer back to discussion of the illustration to confirm or adjust predictions.

In many lessons, the Warm-Up can generate vocabulary lists, semantic webs, or charts of useful information. These can be used and expanded throughout the lesson.

Key Words for Work

Each lesson presents visually three or four words from the conversation or reading. If the words are new to students, use them in sentences to provide context. If students know the words or related ones, have them use the words in sentences. Whenever possible, encourage students to find concrete examples of objects, to demonstrate actions, and to discuss workplaces and other settings in which the key words are used.

Conversation or Reading

Each lesson is organized around a central conversation or reading. The conversations are set in a variety of typical workplaces—offices, clinics, a hotel, a diner, retail businesses, and manufacturers. The readings present common workplace forms or documents.

The conversations and readings model language that ESL students need to succeed in the workplace. They develop the central topic of the lesson. They also let students discuss expected workplace behavior and analyze relationships between characters.

Each conversation or reading is also recorded on the *On-the-Job English* audiotape, which can be played as many times as desired. By listening to the conversations, students can hear how tone affects meaning and develop listening skills. The oral version of readings can reinforce comprehension. The audiotape also lets students hear natural speech.

Students can act out the conversations or create new conversations modeled on the ones in the book. These new conversations can reflect students' own jobs or expand on relationships between characters.

Tips

A set of Tips accompanies each conversation or reading. The Tips will help students carry out the task presented in a conversation or use the document presented in a reading. It can be useful for students to review the Tips before hearing the conversation or reading the document. This lets them listen for the Tips in action or identify where they could use the Tips themselves.

Check Your Understanding

Check Your Understanding is a two-part section. The first part is a short-answer exercise to check literal comprehension of the conversation or reading. Students should be prepared to explain their responses and identify details that back up their answers.

The second part moves students from facts or details to more analytic comprehension of the conversation or reading. For example, they may be asked why things happen in certain ways. They may be prompted to examine words and phrases that indicate relationships in a workplace. They may be asked to express their opinions or to evaluate issues explored in a conversation. Or they may be asked to put themselves in the situation and decide how they would act. Students are also asked to analyze how characters use (or fail to use) the Tips and to consider how the Tips can be useful.

Reinforcement Activities

A variety of activities reinforce the topic and language of the lessons. In some activities, students practice and expand key language functions, for example, by asking questions to clarify information or by filling in a form. In others, students practice key language features through, for example, a contextualized grammar exercise or a rephrasing task.

Try It Out

In Try It Out, a task-based activity helps students begin to apply new skills in work contexts. For instance, students may conduct interviews or role-play workplace interactions. Most activities are done in pairs or small groups, because that is how work is typically organized in many companies. Working collaboratively with others lets students expand their interpersonal and teamwork skills.

Wrap-Up

Each lesson ends with a two-part Wrap-Up. The first part, Understanding Workplace Culture, lets students explore an aspect of U.S. work culture that may be new or confusing. Students may also discuss how work culture in the United States compares to that in their native countries.

In the second part, Application, students use the core language and skills they have learned. Often, the activities, which focus on personal experience and needs, are done outside the classroom. Students bring or report their results to the class and create class charts, booklets, or other documentation of their work.

Adapting Lessons to Specific Workplace Settings

On-the-Job English is designed to apply to any workplace so that students from different jobs can work together in the same class. While the lessons are set in specific workplaces, the skills and functions taught can be used in many different work settings. This is particularly important because most workers in this country cannot expect to stay in one job for a lifetime. To succeed in the American workplace, ESL students need transferable language skills as much as they need transferable employment skills.

There are several ways to customize the lessons. After a particular function or task is presented and discussed, you can ask students how that function or task is done in their workplace. In many lessons, activities and questions provide ways to apply lesson content to students' own jobs. So do some activities suggested in the Lesson Notes. If this is done regularly, students will think of ways to apply new language and skills to their own workplaces whenever a new topic is presented.

Another customizing technique is to help students rewrite a conversation or reading using the vocabulary of their own job. For example, in Lesson 15, "Understanding Announcements," have students bring in sample announcements from their jobs or unions. In pairs or groups, they can find information to substitute in the announcements in the lesson. (e.g., "Training Oppys. at [Their Company]: Sign up in [Their Union Hall]"). The Lesson Notes include some specific suggestions for such adaptations. You can also customize practice activities by having students substitute their own work vocabulary in items.

Finally, be alert to opportunities to have students bring in written workplace materials—instructions, newsletters, announcements, forms, etc.—that relate to the lesson topic. This approach is particularly relevant in lessons that deal with workplace documents, but it can be used for other lessons as well. Concrete examples help bring about useful and permanent learning.

Useful Additions to Lesson Material

A Personal Dictionary: Students can make their own dictionaries in a spiral notebook or a three-ring binder to help them expand their vocabulary and improve their spelling. Have them label each page with a letter of the alphabet. Then have them record the key words and other new words on the correct page, along with a sentence using each word in context. Students can also develop specialized vocabulary pages related to their job, their family, their hobbies, and other topics.

Class Photos, Videos, and Audio Recordings: Photos, videos, and audio recordings are useful and fun ways to record students using the skills they are learning. Be sure to get permission from students beforehand, especially if you intend to use the photos or recordings anywhere else.

Audio recordings are especially useful for students who are practicing or developing conversations. They can also help you diagnose pronunciation difficulties or record progress.

SCANS Correlations to *On-the-Job English* Lessons

The following chart will help you identify and find SCANS Competencies (C1–20) and Foundations Skills (F1–17) that are addressed in *On-the-Job English*. Using this chart, you can make explicit to students the skills and competencies that they are mastering, and you can identify ways to reinforce previously practiced skills in later lessons.

A ✓ next to a number means that the skill listed is a major focus of that lesson.

Lesson	Competencies	Foundation Skills
1	✓ C-5 Acquires and Evaluates Information C-9 Participates as a Member of a Team	✓ F-5 Listening F-10 Seeing Things in the Mind's Eye F-11 Knowing How to Learn
2	✓ C-5 Acquires and Evaluates Information C-6 Organizes and Maintains Information C-10 Teaches Others C-16 Monitors and Corrects Performance	✓ F-6 Speaking F-10 Seeing Things in the Mind's Eye
3	C-5 Acquires and Evaluates Information C-6 Organizes and Maintains Information C-14 Works with Cultural Diversity	✓ F-1 Reading
4	C-1 Allocates Time ✓ C-7 Interprets and Communicates Information C-10 Teaches Others	✓ F-6 Speaking F-13 Responsibility
5	✓ C-6 Organizes and Maintains Information ✓ C-7 Interprets and Communicates Information C-11 Serves Clients/Customers	✓ F-2 Writing F-3 Arithmetic
6	C-3 Allocates Material and Facility Resources C-6 Organizes and Maintains Information C-14 Works with Cultural Diversity C-20 Maintains and Troubleshoots Technology	✓ F-1 Reading
7	C-3 Allocates Material and Facility Resources C-6 Organizes and Maintains Information C-19 Applies Technology to Task	F-13 Responsibility F-15 Social
8	C-3 Allocates Material and Facility Resources C-6 Organizes and Maintains Information C-16 Monitors and Corrects Performance C-20 Maintains and Troubleshoots Technology	F-2 Writing ✓ F-5 Listening ✓ F-6 Speaking F-9 Problem Solving
9	C-3 Allocates Material and Facility Resources C-4 Allocates Human Resources C-12 Exercises Leadership C-16 Monitors and Corrects Performance	F-1 Reading ✓ F-5 Listening F-6 Speaking ✓ F-8 Decision Making F-13 Responsibility

10	C-4 Allocates Human Resources C-9 Participates as a Member of a Team C-10 Teaches Others C-12 Exercises Leadership C-15 Understands Systems	✓ F-8 Decision Making ✓ F-13 Responsibility F-15 Social ✓ F-16 Self-Management

11	✓ C-9 Participates as a Member of a Team
	  C-10 Teaches Others
	  C-13 Negotiates to Arrive at a Decision
	  C-16 Monitors and Corrects Performance
		✓ F-5 Listening
		  F-6 Speaking
		  F-7 Creative Thinking
		  F-15 Social

12	✓ C-9 Participates as a Member of a Team
	  C-11 Serves Clients/Customers
	✓ C-12 Exercises Leadership
	  C-13 Negotiates to Arrive at a Decision
		✓ F-6 Speaking
		  F-15 Social

13	C-4 Allocates Human Resources
	C-6 Organizes and Maintains Information
	C-9 Participates as a Member of a Team
	C-10 Teaches Others
	✓ C-16 Monitors and Corrects Performance
		✓ F-5 Listening
		✓ F-6 Speaking
		  F-8 Decision Making
		  F-14 Self-Esteem
		✓ F-15 Social
		  F-16 Self-Management
		  F-17 Integrity/Honesty

14	✓ C-1 Allocates Time
	✓ C-5 Acquires and Evaluates Information
		✓ F-1 Reading
		  F-7 Creative Thinking
		✓ F-13 Responsibility
		  F-16 Self-Management

15	✓ C-5 Acquires and Evaluates Information
	  C-6 Organizes and Maintains Information
	  C-7 Interprets and Communicates Information
		✓ F-1 Reading
		  F-8 Decision Making
		  F-9 Problem Solving
		  F-11 Knowing How to Learn

16	✓ C-5 Acquires and Evaluates Information
	  C-6 Organizes and Maintains Information
	  C-7 Interprets and Communicates Information
		✓ F-1 Reading
		✓ F-8 Decision Making
		  F-11 Knowing How to Learn

17	C-6 Organizes and Maintains Information C-7 Interprets and Communicates Information	✓ F-1 Reading
18	C-7 Interprets and Communicates Information C-11 Serves Clients/Customers	✓ F-2 Writing ✓ F-5 Listening

Skills and Tasks for Jobs: A SCANS Report for America 2000, The Secretary's Commission on Achieving Necessary Skills, U.S. Department of Labor, Washington, D.C., 1991.

Lesson Notes

Unit 1

Lesson 1: Understanding Spoken Instructions

Workers must understand and follow spoken instructions to learn new jobs and new tasks. To use spoken instructions fully, they must be prepared to ask questions, verify what they were told, and understand the reasons for instructions. They need to understand that asking questions is acceptable and even encouraged in the American workplace.

Warm-Up (page 8)

Experience: Ask students about their work skills and about their skills beyond work, such as carpentry or cooking. Have students talk about where, how, and from whom they learned those skills. List responses on the board. Encourage students to compare learning work skills and learning skills outside of work.

Picture: Elicit and record ideas from students about the setting, the people, and any equipment or gear they can identify. For example, they may recognize the safety gear. Record their predictions of what the two characters are doing and saying.

Key Words: Relate pictures to students' experience. For example, ask if anyone uses a logbook. Compare it to other types of logs, such as check registers.

Conversation and Tips (page 9)

Read the introduction to students. Compare the situation described to the predictions they made in the Warm-Up. Introduce the Tips, and tell students to listen for ways they are used in the conversation. Then listen to the tape of the conversation twice. The second time, have students circle new words. Elicit explanations, or teach the words. Ask general questions (e.g., *What is Mike doing? What is Sonia's new task?*) Point out and review the use of the sequence words *first* and *then.* Then use Part A of the exercise on page 10 to reinforce comprehension of details.

Check Your Understanding (page 10)

Discuss the Questions: As students respond, help them relate their answers to specific language in the conversation. Focus on the relationship between Sonia and Mike. Have students find sentences or phrases that indicate what the relationship is and that show Sonia is comfortable learning from Mike. In question 6, review and discuss the Tips. Then have students identify when and how Sonia used the Tips in the conversation.

Asking Questions about a Job (page 11)

This activity and the next one help learners practice clarifying spoken instructions. Review question words (*who, what, when, why, where, how*) and the kind of answer each word gets.

Individually or in pairs, have students write questions about the instructions and share them with the class. Record and compare the questions. Then have students find answers in the conversation. If they can't answer a question, ask them to discuss what information they would need to do so. Encourage students to formulate other questions about Sonia's task, particularly *why* questions (e.g., "Why do the edges have to be smooth?")

Another Way to Say It (page 11)

This exercise helps learners recognize and use common ways to confirm or clarify details. As a class, identify the function of each sentence. Encourage pairs or groups to brainstorm several other ways to say the same thing. Then have them share their ideas with the class. Have pairs role-play the conversation between Sonia and Mike, using some of the new expressions.

Try It Out (page 12)

Give and Follow Instructions: Review the shapes listed, and have volunteers draw examples on the board. Elicit and record the names of objects with those shapes. Review prepositions of place (*under, on, around,* etc.).

Divide the class into two teams. Have each team read and discuss one of the sets of instructions. Then form pairs with one member from each team to complete the exercise. Each drawing may be different.

Share Your Drawings: Have students point out differences and discuss why and how they occurred. Have them try to rewrite the instructions so each set elicits only one result.

Discuss the Question: Help students contrast tasks in which results must be uniform (e.g., manufacturing) and those in which variations are acceptable (e.g., housecleaning).

Wrap-Up (page 13)

Culture: Have students read and discuss Mike's message. Review idioms (*up front, take time*). As students discuss the questions, ask them to compare Mike's attitude with that of supervisors they have worked for. Stress that it is common and even expected in the American workplace for workers to ask questions. Discuss similarities and differences between these norms and those in students' native countries.

Application: As students respond to the questions, encourage them to discuss whether they feel comfortable asking questions at work and why. Point out that issues in question 2 will be explored in Lesson 2.

Lesson 2: Giving Spoken Instructions

Workers frequently give spoken instructions to co-workers or to people they supervise. To do this successfully, students must learn to think through the steps in a task and put them in order. They should know how to use signal words for sequential steps (*first, next, then, last*) and simultaneous steps (*as, as soon as, at the same time as, during, while*). They must also be prepared to respond to questions and to check that the instructions have been understood.

Warm-Up (page 14)

Experience: Point out that people give instructions to others all the time. For example, they teach children how to tie shoelaces, they tell a friend how to prepare food, or they give a delivery person directions to their home. Remind students of their answers to question 2 in Application, page 13. Elicit and record a list of instructions that students have given.

Picture: Elicit predictions of who the people are, what their roles are, what is happening, and why. Record the reasons suggested by students. Ask if any students have used similar equipment, and if so, for what tasks.

Conversation and Tips (page 15)

After students listen to the conversation, review any new vocabulary. Compare students' predictions to the information in the conversation, and discuss words or phrases that show the relationship between Janet and Wang.

Ask about Wang's attitude toward cleaning up. Refer back to the reasons students gave in the Warm-Up, and compare them to the reason Janet gives. Discuss the importance of cleaning and maintaining tools and how students do this in their jobs or at home.

After looking at the Tips, have students review the conversation to see how Wang asks clarifying questions, how Janet answers the questions, and how Janet checks for understanding.

Check Your Understanding (page 16)

Review the Information: If students are unsure of an answer, discuss ways to revise and clarify Janet's instructions.

Discuss the Questions: After students respond to question 3, elicit phrases or sentences that ask whether instructions are understood (e.g., "Is that clear? Do you follow?").

Using Sequence Words (page 17)

Use a time line to demonstrate sequence. Write *start* at one end and *end* at the other. Ask where on the line students would put the sequence words *first, second, last,* etc. Point out that some words, such as *next, then,* or *after that,* can be anywhere in a sequence (except for the first step). Give some oral instructions with sequence words, and have a student carry them out (e.g., *"First, stand up. Then, walk to the board. Next, write your name."*) Then let that student give similar instructions to another student.

Giving Clear Instructions (page 17)

Put the Steps in Order: Remind students to think out all the steps before giving instructions.

Students can trade instructions with several partners. (Be sure they recheck the order each time they trade with a different partner.) After students put the steps in order, have them give the instructions orally, using sequence words. Or have them rewrite the instructions, combining steps and using sequence words and subordinate clauses to show sequence.

Using Tools: In this section, students practice giving clear instructions. The exercise also reinforces the importance of caring for tools.

Try It Out (page 18)

Divide the class into two teams. Have each team read and discuss one of the forms, clarifying vocabulary and actions. Then form pairs with one member from each team for the activity. Remind the listeners not to look at the written instructions. Tell the readers that they may have to explain or spell some words. After students have finished, discuss jobs or situations that might require changing sandpaper or draining pipes.

Wrap-Up (page 19)

Culture: Prompt students with other examples if they have trouble starting their lists. (For example, for List 1, people speak quickly, rush from step to step, don't look at you, or don't check if you understand. For List 2, people speak slowly, make eye contact, or ask you to repeat the instructions to confirm understanding.)

Application: Discussing these questions encourages empathy and helps students become more confident in teaching and learning tasks. By discussing question 2, students learn different ways to give clear instructions and to ask for clarification when receiving instructions.

Lesson Extension

Have students role-play giving and receiving instructions. They can follow the structure of the conversation on page 15 and substitute terms and steps from their own jobs or experience (e.g., "Wang is training to be a *machinist*." "Before you do anything, check the *fluid level*.") Or they can follow the simple process they used in Giving Clear Instructions, Part A (page 17).

Lesson 3: Using Written Instructions

Workers often need to comprehend and respond to written instructions. These instructions may be in list or paragraph form or in formal or informal language. Workers must also understand and use pictures and diagrams. Remind students that they can and should ask questions if written instructions are unclear.

Warm-Up (page 20)

Experience: Ask if students ever follow recipes, write travel directions for a friend, or leave notes telling family members what to do. Point out that in all these examples they are using written directions. Ask students for other examples. Ask where they have used pictures or diagrams to help them follow written directions (e.g., using the + and – signs on a diagram to determine the correct way to insert batteries).

Picture: Discuss the work setting in this picture. Ask who is familiar with a vacuum cleaner or any other machine with a part that is changed periodically. Remind students of the electric sander in Try It Out, page 18.

Key Words: Elicit and record a list of machines with power switches (almost all household appliances, power tools, computers, etc.).

Reading and Tips (page 21)

Read the introduction with students. Then have students read the instructions and look at the pictures. Review any new vocabulary. Discuss how the pictures clarify the instructions. Review the Tips. Ask students how they could check their work if they were following these instructions. As follow-up, listen to the tape, and have students identify ways in which the oral instructions differ from the written ones (e.g., use of *Step* before each number).

Extension: Have students turn the numbered instructions into paragraph form. Bring in other examples of written instructions, and have groups of students rewrite them in a different format (e.g., change paragraphs to numbered lists; change formal language to informal).

Check Your Understanding (page 22)

Discuss the Questions: After discussing question 1, ask other *why* questions about the steps in the reading (e.g., *"Why do you clean the filter every time you change the dust bag?"*). Encourage students to guess if the answer is not explicit.

Follow the Steps in Order (page 23)

Encourage students to complete the exercise from memory individually or in pairs and then refer to the reading to confirm their answers.

Using Action Words (page 23)

Have students act out the words in the box (e.g., *"Frank, shake something. Anna, remove something from the desk."*) Remind students that instructions are usually written in the imperative—they give commands. After students complete the exercise, elicit and record other common instruction words used with machines (e.g., *push, take off, put on, install, insert*).

Scanning Written Instructions (page 24)

Give students one or two pages from a newspaper, or use the student book's table of contents. Ask them to find a particular story or piece of information as quickly as possible by scanning headlines or lesson titles. Remind students that *scan,* as used here, means to read very quickly. Then discuss how they found the information. Stress the difference between scanning and close reading.

Read the activity introduction and directions with the class. Set a time limit (one or two minutes) for students to scan the reading and complete the activity. Check answers together.

Extension: Bring in copies of want ads or catalog pages. Have students take turns picking an ad or catalog entry, describing it, and having the rest of the class scan to find it. If you use catalog pages, discuss how pictures can help in scanning.

Try It Out (page 24)

Demonstrate how to use the yellow pages, or allow students to demonstrate. Discuss the kinds of information found in it. If necessary, work on alphabetizing skills as well. Then have students work in pairs to complete the activity and compare answers with other pairs.

Wrap-Up (page 25)

Culture: Have students look at the example and generate a list of questions they can ask to elicit the information (e.g., "What written instructions do you use at work? What job tasks have you learned from written instructions? Who do you write instructions for at home? Have you ever written a reminder to someone in your house? What was it for?"). Role-play with a volunteer to demonstrate how to conduct an interview. (The volunteer can respond with the information in the example.) Then have students interview each other (or, if they wish to do the activity outside of class, co-workers or friends). Make sure students understand how to fill in the chart. Point out that they should record responses during the interview or as soon as they finish it.

Application: Explain that students can bring in instructions that they have used or that they have seen at work or in their neighborhood. If necessary, first have them brainstorm examples.

Lesson 4: Describing Results

Workers are frequently required to report the work they have completed to supervisors or to co-workers. Students must be able to explain clearly and concisely what work has been completed and what still needs to be done. This includes specifying quantities accurately.

Warm-Up (page 26)

Experience: Ask students to name some of the steps you carry out at the beginning of class (e.g., reviewing notes from a previous class, checking homework, asking students what they've done since the last class). Explain that those tasks help you determine what needs to be done in class. Point out that other types of workers also need to find out what has happened and what needs to be done before starting a job. Have students discuss the information they need as they start their work each day.

Picture: Discuss where the people are and what they might be saying. Ask how workers know when it's time to restock materials at their jobs.

Conversation and Tips (page 27)

After students listen to the conversation, ask broad comprehension questions. Be sure to include questions that show how the Tips were applied (e.g., *"How does the health clinic let its workers know what needs to be done? Did Albert finish everything on the work order? What does he tell Lourdes about work he completed? How does Albert let Lourdes know what she still needs to do?"*). Discuss how Lourdes gets additional information about what she needs to do.

Check Your Understanding (page 28)

Discuss the Questions: In discussing Albert and Lourdes's relationship, point out their casual, friendly tone; Albert's restocking of the cart for Lourdes; and her expression of appreciation.

Using Time Expressions (page 29)

Review expressions that signal past or future time. Point out that time expressions can be less or more specific. Some might refer to a particular month or week *(during the past week, in a few weeks)*; some to particular day *(last Tuesday; tomorrow)*; and some to a particular hour or minute *(at sunset last Tuesday; as soon as you get in tomorrow morning)*.

Have students look at the calendar on page 29 and find March 16. Let them guess which dates are meant by the phrases in the box. After they complete the exercise, have them generate lists of other words and phrases that show past and future time.

Try It Out (page 30)

Asking Questions: Stress the importance of asking questions to pinpoint what work has been completed and what still needs to be done. After students complete the activity, look at different questions that can elicit the same answer (e.g., "Do I have to order anything?" vs. "How many cartons of gloves should I order?"). Discuss when each would be used.

Using Quantity Terms: After students conduct their interviews, chart the results on the board. Discuss the responses collected. Have students distinguish terms for specific measurements *(a gallon, a liter)* from terms for containers, whose meanings can vary. (e.g., A *carton* of milk could contain a quart or a half-gallon; a *carton* of eggs could contain a dozen; a *carton* of copy paper could contain eight packages of 500 sheets each.)

Wrap-Up (page 31)

Culture: After students read the report, ask them what sort of company this is. Review new or idiomatic vocabulary (e.g., *tally, boosted*). Discuss the tone of the report, noting such phrases as *I'm thrilled to report*. In discussing the questions, students may wish to compare practices in the U.S. with those in their native countries. If appropriate, students can write a similar report noting achievements of class members (e.g., getting a job or promotion, completing a training program, passing a test).

Application: After students compare the results of their interviews, they can group the types of information people have to report (e.g., results, accomplishments, problems) and discuss why those things are reported on a regular basis.

Lesson Extension

Have students practice describing results. Ask them to use their own workplace as the setting for a conversation modeled after the one on page 27.

Lesson 5: Documenting Results

Documentation of work is increasingly important in American workplaces. Good documentation benefits others in an organization, such as other team members, the next shift, or other departments. Students need to understand the role of documentation. They must be able to provide clear, concise reports, with accurate numbers where required.

Warm-Up (page 32)

Experience: Bring in and ask students to bring in samples of work documentation: logbooks, computer entries, tags, receipts, etc. You can also bring in charts or graphs from newspapers or magazines. Discuss and list the kinds of records your students must keep at work. Talk about similarities and differences across jobs. Then discuss and list some reasons that people keep personal records (calculating taxes, verifying that bills were paid, tracking household spending, etc.).

Chart: Examine the chart, and ask who is familiar with this kind of chart. Ask for volunteers to discuss when, why, and how they've used such charts.

Reading and Tips (page 33)

Read the introduction and Tips together. Point out that some work records are long-term (e.g., kept for a month, a year, or longer) and some are short term (e.g., given to the next shift). Point out that most companies require workers to use established formats to report information (e.g., this chart). Discuss and demonstrate how to read the chart across and down. Review special vocabulary *(urgent, special order, back order)* and quantity words *(gross, dozen, foot)*, referring back to page 32 if appropriate. Play the tape to reinforce the details and any new vocabulary.

Then ask students about information on the chart (e.g., *"What time did Raul make a delivery to Paula Santos? Why are there no initials or time for the delivery to Omar and Melrose?"*). Review the Tips, and discuss why records need to be accurate. Ask students how they check any records they keep for accuracy and completeness.

Check Your Understanding (page 34)

Review the Information: Review scanning techniques from Lesson 3 (page 24), and encourage students to scan for the answers to this activity.

Discuss the Questions: If students have trouble answering question 6, prompt with such questions as *"Who do you think cares about the back orders that Raul notes? How could the production department use this information?"*

Finding and Using Details (page 35)

What Do the Headings Mean? Discuss the column headings, and ask why those details on deliveries are important. Review the use of question words *(who, what, when, where, how much/how many)*. Write the words on the board. Ask, *"What word would I use if I wanted to know someone's name? The number of students in this class? The country you came from?"* etc. Write each response under the appropriate word so that students can see

the relationships. Have students complete the exercise individually or in pairs.

Figure Mileage and Cost: Ask students why it is important for a delivery person to keep a tally of miles. Discuss who in Raul's company would use this information. Ask why there is a difference between the ending mileage of one day and the starting mileage of the next day. Then go over how students would figure out the daily mileage totals and the weekly tally. Do the first one together, then let individuals or pairs complete the tallies and figure the weekly expense for the shift.

Extension: Have students keep a weekly tally of the mileage on their own cars or of their bus or train expenses. They can keep records of their travel to work or to class. More advanced students can keep records of all trips and then categorize them for work, for school, for entertainment, etc. Using their week's tallies, students can then chart and calculate educational or job-related travel expenses for those who travel by bus or train and mileage for those who use cars. They can also calculate expenses for car travel, using a standard per-mile cost (e.g., $.25) and including costs for tolls or parking.

Try It Out (page 36)

Read the directions together. Review the column headings, and discuss who would use a chart like this. Then let pairs of students decide what is missing. Go over the missing information as a group. Elicit possible reasons for the gaps.

Let students read the roles they will each play, select a name for their character, and think about what they want to say. Then have each pair create a conversation and perform it for the class. Record suggestions made in the conversations for improving the salesperson's record keeping. Discuss whether students could use any of the ideas in their own jobs.

Wrap-Up (page 37)

Culture: Discuss various kinds of documentation. Have students identify the questions that elicited the information in the example. (You could also role-play the process with a volunteer.) Let students interview each other and record information in class before they interview people outside.

Discuss any problems they have asking questions or recording responses. Be sure they are not overly concerned with spelling or with writing whole sentences.

Application: When the interviews are completed, give teams time to discuss their findings and respond to the questions.

Extension: Encourage teams to prepare a report of their findings for the rest of the class. Have them decide on an appropriate format (e.g., preparing a master chart, reporting orally or in writing, role-playing a reporter interviewing several workers). Then have teams present their reports to the class.

Lesson Extension

Review the use of capital letters and abbreviations, using examples from the charts in the lesson. Discuss why capital letters are important in such documents and why abbreviations are used.

Unit 1 Review (page 38)

Point out that this activity deals with idiomatic expressions used many workplaces. Refer students to the similar rewriting exercise on page 11. If students ask about the meaning of any item, refer to the conversation, reading, or exercise on which the sentence is based. Note and contrast the different meanings of *check* in numbers 2 and 3. Encourage students to share idiomatic expressions from their jobs and discuss how to put those expressions into more formal language.

Unit 2

Lesson 6: Using Safety Gear

Safety gear refers to any clothing and equipment that workers use to protect themselves as they work. Students need to recognize different types of safety gear for different jobs and understand the necessity of using appropriate gear.

Warm-Up (page 40)

Experience: Discuss any special clothing that students use at their jobs. Help them distinguish uniforms from protective clothing. Introduce or review the terms *equipment* and *gear* as they are used to refer to safety items and protective clothing. Elicit any other safety gear students use. Ask if it is optional or required and who decides if it will be used. Ask if they used similar gear in their native countries.

Picture: Have students name items they are familiar with. Elicit terms for other safety gear they know, and begin to generate a master list that will be developed throughout the unit.

Conversation and Tips (page 41)

Bring in labels or pictures of labels from various cleaning products or other chemicals used at home (e.g., window cleaner, oven cleaner, insect spray). Have students look at the warning labels and discuss why skin must be protected from these chemicals. Ask if students wear rubber gloves when they use chemical cleaners, and discuss why rubber gloves are important. Ask if there are other ways the chemicals might be unsafe (e.g., fumes).

Read the title and introduction together, and review the Tips. After students listen to the conversation, elicit explanations of any new vocabulary. Look at the Tips again, and discuss the ways Rosa, Leon, and their family members apply them.

Check Your Understanding (page 42)

Review the Information: Each type of gear is associated with one type of worker mentioned in the conversation. Students, however, may recognize that some items are used by more than one type of worker. Those matches should also be

acknowledged as correct and can be reinforced in question 1 of Discuss the Questions.

Discuss the Questions: Use these questions as an opportunity to expand the master vocabulary list of safety gear. For question 5, ask what kind of relationship Rosa and Leon seem to have and what in the conversation shows their relationship. Ask students if they discuss their families with people at work and if so, with whom.

Categorizing (page 43)

Make sure students understand *hazard*. Check understanding of the pictures and words. Elicit examples of sources of the hazards and uses of the gear.

To do this exercise as a class, copy the chart on the board. Have students discuss each choice, and have volunteers write the answers in the correct boxes.

Extension: Extend the exercise by teaching or eliciting words for other body parts, hazards, and protective gear and expanding the chart.

Try It Out (page 44)

Safe or Unsafe? Use this activity to stress that regular clothing, as well as jewelry and hairstyles, can affect safety. Explain any new vocabulary with pictures or examples from class members (e.g., *"Who's wearing a bracelet? Is anyone wearing loose sleeves?"*) Demonstrate how to complete the chart by asking students to select from the list one safe and one unsafe item. Discuss reasons for those choices. Have students work in pairs or small groups to categorize the other items and to generate additional examples from their own jobs or experience. Then have students explain their answers, using their own jobs as reference points. Discuss situations in which responses could differ. For example, point out that long hair, loose sleeves, bracelets, and dangling earrings may be safe around certain machines—fax machine, photocopier, or telephone.

Wrap-Up (page 45)

Culture: Ask students how they care for their gear at work and if they or their co-workers have ever had problems with damaged gear. Record the vocabulary they use (e.g., *oil, wash, polish*). Bring in or have students bring in examples of care instructions for various items (clothes, tools, home appliances, etc.) so the class can discuss the language used. Focus on the use of imperative sentences. In discussing question 3, elicit potential risks of sharing safety gear. Ask if there are rules about sharing gear where students work.

Application: Combine the responses into one class chart of jobs and kinds of safety gear. Students can also group the information in other ways (e.g., by item, which will show the different jobs that use the same gear).

Lesson Extension

Have pairs or groups rewrite the conversation on page 41, using job terminology and examples of safety gear from their workplaces. Have them practice the new conversations and perform them for the class.

Lesson 7: Understanding Rules and Regulations

Rules and regulations in the American workplace cover many different areas, including use of equipment and materials, behavior, and dress. In particular, worker safety requires a clear understanding of company rules and government regulations. To understand what rules and regulations apply and why, students must know what is posted in their workplace and be prepared to ask for explanations when necessary.

Warm-Up (page 46)

Experience: Ask students to think about rules they have to follow at home (e.g., chores for family members) or in the community (e.g., traffic laws). Ask them who makes the rules and if they think it's important to understand the reasons for the rules. Then discuss rules they follow at work and whether or not they know who made those rules and the reasons for them.

Picture: Discuss the signs and their meanings. Ask students which ones they have seen and where.

Key Words: If possible, bring in a first-aid kit to show students the contents. Ask students to locate an alarm pull in the classroom or building.

Reading and Tips (page 47)

Read the title and introduction together, and remind students of Leon's reference to OSHA in Lesson 6. Have students listen to the reading twice, once to make sure they understand any new vocabulary and once to consider and discuss why each policy is important. Note that some policies include both work rules and information on available safety equipment. Ask why they think Sanders Industries has that equipment available. Then review the Tips. Have students imagine they are workers at Sanders Industries and have them create questions to ask a supervisor.

Extension: Elicit other OSHA rules that students know from their jobs. This reading was adapted from OSHA regulations. Discuss what OSHA means for workers. Try to have an OSHA representative come in and talk to your students. If you want more information on OSHA, try the human resources department of a nearby company or your local library.

Check Your Understanding (page 48)

Review the Details: Have students complete the exercise from memory and then scan the reading to check their answers.

Discuss the Questions: In discussing question 1, have students also describe or plan emergency exit routes they can use in their homes. Relate responses to question 3 to the Tips. If appropriate, have students generate questions to ask about their own workplace or describe how they have applied the Tips in their own job. For question 4, ask students how the policies in the reading could apply to their jobs. If students have a similar document from work, encourage them to bring it in and compare it to the reading.

Safety Rules and Reasons (page 49)

Review the rules and the reasons to make sure students understand all vocabulary. Have them complete the exercise independently or in small groups. Then discuss the answers. Ask students if they can think of additional reasons for the rules.

Talking about Safety Rules and Reasons (page 49)

This activity helps students prepare to ask questions so they can understand the reasons behind safety rules and to ask for safety information or protection if they are concerned about risks.

Try It Out (page 50)

What Rule Was Broken? After students complete the activity, review responses as a class and have students explain their answers. Discuss any differences.

Talk about Safety: Have students describe the pictures orally or in writing. The descriptions can then be the basis for role-playing, demonstrating interactions between a supervisor and the workers in the pictures or between co-workers. Discuss differences in the way supervisors or co-workers would talk to the workers in the pictures.

Wrap-Up (page 51)

Culture: Discuss repetitive-motion injuries and back injuries. Present relevant facts, for example: More than 300,000 workers in the U.S. got repetitive-motion injuries in 1995.[1] Back disorders account for 27 percent of all nonfatal occupational injuries and illnesses involving days away from work.[2] Workers' compensation payments for low-back disorders total about $11 billion a year.[3] Talk about what types of workers are most at risk for these injuries. Ask students if they or anyone they know has had such injuries and what happened. Have students focus on ways to prevent these injuries. If possible, bring in information on exercises and other preventive measures.

Application: Create a class display or booklet of safety signs. Group signs under such headings as "Safety on the Job" and "Safety in the Neighborhood." Have students identify signs that give the same message in different ways (e.g., different words, symbols instead of words).

Lesson 8: Following Safety Rules

Workers are expected to recognize and follow rules and warnings posted in their workplaces. Students must understand the importance of following these rules and what could happen if they don't. They should also be prepared to give concise warnings to others about the risks of not following posted rules.

Warm-Up (page 52)

Experience: Review various warning words or phrases that students know (*Watch out! Careful! Don't walk!* etc.). Reinforce the term *warning* with various common signs (*Danger* signs at a construction site, a flashing yellow light, etc.). Talk about situations in which students have warned co-workers, children, or others of danger. Point out that warnings have different degrees of urgency. They can alert someone to immediate danger, or they can explain possible hazards or consequences (as in Jaya's warning in the conversation on page 53 or the labels on chemical cleaners).

Picture: Elicit predictions of what the women are doing and saying and what the problem might be.

Key Words: Relate *face shield* to gear discussed in Lesson 6, and add the term to the master vocabulary list. Ask students to find examples of hinges in the classroom.

Conversation and Tips (page 53)

Have students listen to the conversation and confirm or adjust their predictions. Discuss how Lia tries to persuade Jaya let her continue working and how Jaya responds. Have students work in pairs or groups to develop categories for words in the introduction and conversation (e.g., safety gear, tools, hazards). Use Jaya's explanation of *liable* to show that accidents affect a company as well as an individual.

Check Your Understanding (page 54)

Review the Information: Have students use evidence from the conversation to explain their responses. Have them turn any false statements into true ones.

1. Occupational Safety and Health Administration, "Total Injury and Illness Cases in 1995" [WWW document] URL: http://www.osha-slc.gov/SLTC/Ergonomics/chart4.html (accessed April 7, 1998).
2. National Institute of Occupational Safety and Health, "NORA Priority Research Areas" [WWW document] URL: http://www.cdc.gov/niosh/diseas.html (accessed April 7, 1998).
3. National Institute of Occupational Safety and Health, "Practical Prevention of Musculoskeletal Disorders Highlighted in NIOSH Workplace Primer" [WWW document] URL: http://www.cdc.gov/niosh/musculo.html (last updated May 9, 1997).

Discuss the Questions: Help students analyze the tone as well as the content of the conversation in discussing questions 2 and 3. When discussing how Lia uses or doesn't use the Tips, have students decide what advice they would give her.

Giving and Understanding Warnings (page 55)

Look at Safety Signs: If necessary, do question 1 together as an example. Have students discuss the signs and then create their sentence for each. You can also have them work in pairs or groups to complete the activity.

Make a Safety Sign: Read and discuss the directions and the examples. Make sure students can use key safety terms, such as *warning, caution,* and *danger.* Ask them about signs with a diagonal line that shows something is not allowed (e.g., Do Not Enter, No Food or Drink, No Smoking). They can base their signs on safety concerns at home, at work, at school, etc.

Have students post their signs, and then have other students create captions that tell what the signs mean. Students could also compile the signs in a class safety booklet.

Shout It Out! (page 56)

Discuss the directions and the example. If necessary, review the use of imperative verbs and exclamation marks. Discuss how to react when one hears these warnings. Elicit situations, at work or elsewhere, in which they can be used. Ask students to share other warning shouts they have heard (e.g., *Watch it! Watch out!*), whether or not they understood them.

Try It Out (page 56)

Have students work in pairs or groups to identify and describe the problems in the picture and to create safety rules for the people to follow. Compare responses as a class.

Extension: Have students create conversations or role-play interactions between the people in the picture and a supervisor or co-worker.

Wrap-Up (page 57)

Culture: Have students work in groups to identify Jaya's reasons and discuss the questions. Then have a reporter from each group summarize the

results for the class. Compare differences in responses.

Application: Rewriting the labels lets students focus on the meaning of the complex language commonly used. They may also learn the dangers in some common items.

Lesson Extension

In pairs or small groups, have students rewrite the conversation on page 53, substituting vocabulary and tasks from their own workplaces or referring to conditions in their native countries. Discuss whether supervisors they know would respond as Jaya does, and whether workers would talk to a supervisor as Lia does.

Lesson 9: Safety Problems at Work

Workers must be able to report safety problems promptly, clearly and concisely, and to the right person. Students must understand that reporting safety problems can save health, lives, and money. They need to be aware that follow-up reports—forms, written reports, testimony—may be required. In particular, they need to understand reporting policies that differ from those in their native countries.

Warm-Up (page 58)

Experience: Discuss the questions. Encourage students to talk about workplace injuries or accidents in the U.S. or in their native countries. Keep in mind that students may feel uncomfortable discussing safety problems for fear of losing face or presenting their company in a bad light. If students are not sure who to tell about an accident, help them determine how to find out.

Picture: Ask students to predict what will happen, and record their predictions. (You can go back and review the predictions after listening to the conversation.) Discuss the difference between individual carelessness and unsafe conditions.

Conversation and Tips (page 59)

Review the Tips before listening to the conversation. Relate them to points discussed in the Warm-Up. Tell students to pay attention to how the characters follow the Tips. Make sure students understand who the characters are and that Subra is reporting what he saw. Then play the tape.

Ask students to summarize the events in a chain activity. For example, start with the sentence, *"First, Jaime was carrying some big boxes."* Then let volunteers add sentences that review the sequence of events. Record the sentences on the board, and have students verify their order.

Discuss the feelings expressed in the conversation: concern ("Will Jaime be OK?"), worry ("Will I get in trouble?"), etc. Remind students of the discussion of liability in Lesson 8. Ask about Irina's attitude. Discuss if she is sympathetic to Jaime, concerned about the company, or both.

Check Your Understanding (page 60)

Review the Information: Remind students not to draw unsupported conclusions from incomplete information. For example, they can't conclude that Jaime broke his arm just because Subra says he fell on it and yelled.

Adding Important Facts (page 61)

Discuss the importance of reporting and documenting details about safety problems. Let students respond individually and then work as a class or in small groups to review and compare responses. Ask students to explain their reasons for including or excluding a detail.

Understanding Warning Signs (page 61)

This activity pulls together work on the meaning of warning signs and of verbal warnings. Refer to activities in preceding lessons for review and preparation.

Try It Out (page 62)

Filling Out an Accident Report: This activity requires students to sift through the expanded language of an oral description, find details, and turn them into the concise form required for a report. They have to decide which points from the conversation are essential and which are not.

Asking for More Information: In this activity, students have to consider what other information is required for such a report (e.g., time, location, treatment) and how they can ask for it.

Wrap-Up (page 63)

Culture: After students bring in responses, create a class chart to compare the information. Encourage them to ask for and bring in accident report forms, if possible.

Application: Have the teams representing Jaime (the injured worker) and Irina (the supervisor) separately discuss what happened from the perspective of their character and prepare to describe the accident. Then have each team present its position to the mediating team. Have the mediators decide what Jaime should do and explain their position. Then ask the teams representing Jaime and Irina to express their reactions to the decision. Discuss why time away from work can cost money to both an individual and a company. If possible, bring in or ask students to bring in copies of workers' compensation and disability policies from their workplaces. Review and compare them.

Unit 2 Review (page 64)

This activity requires students to review safety rules and regulations and general safety practices. After students correct the sentences, have them explain reasons for the correct version and discuss why the original is incorrect.

Unit 3

Lesson 10: Understanding Roles and Responsibilities

As workplace culture changes, workers need to understand the increasing importance of leadership and teamwork skills. Students need to develop those skills, to understand how decisions are made, and to understand how people relate and communicate in organizations.

Warm-Up (page 66)

Experience: Have students begin to consider how their workplace is organized and their position in it. This will prepare them to discuss the chart. Ask who makes decisions about tasks at work and how much leeway they have in how they do things.

Chart: Have students discuss their own positions at work and who they know in other positions. Discuss how people move up in organizations and what students can do to move up.

Key Words: Discuss the activities typically carried out at a central office and at branch stores. If your program has a similar structure, use the comparison to clarify meaning.

Conversation and Tips (page 67)

Make sure students understand that there are three characters and two conversations. Listen to and discuss each conversation separately. After the first, discuss what Rudy did wrong and what problem he created. After the second, discuss Greta's response to the problem and how it compares to Mr. Ford's. Discuss why Greta tells Rudy about Cathy Blaine's promotion.

Check Your Understanding (page 68)

Discuss the Questions: In question 3, ask students what Rudy could do if he faces this situation again (e.g., ask a friend or relative to pick up his children, arrange with Greta for a teammate to write up the tallies). In question 5, ask students to find similarities and differences in the conversations between Rudy and Mr. Ford and between Rudy and Greta. From this comparison, discuss the

ways people on different organizational levels relate to each other (e.g., Rudy is more formal with Mr. Ford).

Using Two-Word Verbs (page 69)

Review the verbs in the box. Demonstrate how to read a sentence and substitute a verb from the box for the underlined one. Then check off the verb selected to eliminate it from the list. Have students complete the exercise individually or in pairs.

Extension: Teach other two-word verbs common in work situations: *hold up, keep at, give up, calm down, zero in, put off, move over, blow up,* etc.

What Makes a Good Leader? (page 69)

Review the directions. Discuss the column headings and the examples. Elicit one or two other examples for each column to make sure students understand *effective*. Point out that there are no right or wrong answers. Ask students to talk or write about people they know who demonstrate the leadership qualities listed in each column.

Try It Out (page 70)

Talking to a Co-Worker: Divide the class into Team A and Team B. Read the directions together, then let each team read and discuss its part. Pair members from each team to do the activity.

Talking to a Supervisor: Have pairs alternate taking the roles of the co-workers and the role of the supervisor (shared by the members of a pair). Encourage pairs to perform their conversations. As a class, compare different solutions recommended by the co-workers or the supervisors.

Evaluate the Conversations: Students can refer to the lists of qualities created on page 69.

Wrap-Up (page 71)

Culture: To prepare for the interview, have students suggest questions they can ask to get the information in the chart. Record the questions on the board. Then have volunteers use the example responses to model an interview. When students have completed the exercise, have them discuss the results in groups. Have the groups report the most interesting or unexpected responses.

Application: Refer to the chart on page 66. Bring in examples of organizational charts, or make one for an organization students are familiar with. Then have them create organizational charts of their own workplaces.

Lesson 11: Asking for and Offering Help

Some students may be reluctant to ask for or offer help, because of language difficulties or because such actions are frowned on in their native culture. This reluctance can create misunderstanding in the American workplace. Students need to learn appropriate ways to interrupt co-workers or supervisors, to ask for help, and to indicate the urgency of their request. They also need to express polite appreciation and their own willingness to help others.

Warm-Up (page 72)

Experience: If students seem reluctant to respond, offer examples of times you have asked for help. Discuss how people feel when they have to ask for help and when they can offer help. Encourage students to discuss differences between American workers and workers in their native countries. Stress that it is acceptable to ask for help when needed, that it is better to ask for help than to do something incorrectly.

Picture: Ask students to predict what is happening and what the women's roles are. Ask how they can tell how the women feel.

Conversation and Tips (page 73)

Make sure students understand that there are three characters: Peggy, a new worker in the dining room; Nia, the dining room supervisor; and Mary, an experienced worker. Review the Tips before playing the tape. Tell students to pay attention to the responses Peggy gets when she follows the Tips and when she doesn't. After students listen to the tape, discuss those responses. Ask students to contrast the way Peggy requests help from Nia and from Mary. Consider reasons for the difference.

Which Would You Say? (page 75)

Talk about polite and impolite ways to say something. Use examples from the conversation on page 73 to identify ways that a person can be polite or impolite, helpful or unhelpful. Discuss how the differences can come from words or tone. For each item in the activity, ask students who might be having the conversation: co-workers, supervisor and subordinate, or customer and worker. After students choose the better response for each, have them explain specifically what makes one choice better (more polite, more helpful) than the other.

What Are They Really Saying? (page 75)

Students may want to reread the conversation on page 73 or listen to it again for this exercise. After they rewrite the sentences, have volunteers read their sentences aloud and confirm that the meaning is the same.

Try It Out (page 76)

Asking for Help: Do the activity in two steps. First have students explain or identify the request and brainstorm different ways to make it. Then have students put their alternate versions on the board and evaluate them for meaning, clarity, and politeness. Discuss which of the suggestions would be appropriate when talking to different people (e.g., supervisors, friends, customers, co-workers).

Asking for More Help: Have students use the techniques discussed so far in the lesson in the conversation they create.

Extension: Encourage students to create different forms of the conversation, demonstrating different degrees of politeness, willingness to help, etc.

Wrap-Up (page 77)

After creating the lists in Understanding Workplace Culture and expanding them in Application, encourage students to use ideas generated in these activities to discuss what they can say or do differently at work.

Lesson 12: Expressing Opinions

To participate fully in the American workplace, workers must explain ideas, make suggestions, and evaluate procedures. They must be able to express opinions on many different subjects in team meetings and in everyday encounters. Students need to learn to express ideas confidently and in culturally appropriate ways.

Warm-Up (page 78)

Experience: If students are uncomfortable responding to the questions, give examples from your own experience. Ask if they have ever seen or heard anything similar. Encourage them to compare the way Americans disagree (at work or in other situations) with the way people in their native country disagree.

Picture: Elicit predictions about the people, their jobs, and their relationship. Discuss clues to how well they are getting along (expressions, body language, etc.).

Conversation and Tips (page 79)

Read the introduction together so students understand there are three characters: a waitress, a male cook, and a male manager. Instruct students to pay attention to the differences in the way the three people make and respond to suggestions. After listening to the conversation, discuss the problem, how the three characters make their points, and how they react to each other's ideas. Review the Tips. Elicit students' ideas on how the Tips can enhance relations with co-workers.

Check Your Understanding (page 80)

Discuss the Questions: As students discuss the questions, ask if they think the conversation could have been more effective, and if so, what they would say or do differently.

Making and Responding to Suggestions (page 81)

Offer or Turn Down a Suggestion? To model ways to offer or turn down a suggestion, refer to the conversation on page 79. Gino gives a suggestion that Erik rejects. Have students find those sentences. Then have students complete the exercise individually or in pairs. When reviewing responses, have students discuss the degree of politeness in each statement.

Weak, Assertive, or Aggressive: Make sure students understand the meanings of *weak, assertive,* and *aggressive.* Stress that these words describe a range of behavior. Let students do this exercise individually. Then have them review the answers in small groups. Point out that opinions may differ in this activity. If so, let students explain their

categorization of the statements. For additional practice, have them categorize the statements in Part A in the same way.

Try It Out (page 82)

Disagreeing with People: This activity contrasts polite but assertive ways and rude or offensive ways of expressing opinions. In pairs, let students match poor and respectful ways of saying the same thing. Have students share their own examples of poor and respectful statements. Record the examples on the board, and let students decide which they think are the most useful, the most polite, the rudest, etc. Suggest that they copy down any ones they like.

Wrap-Up (page 83)

Culture: Divide the class into small groups to discuss questions 1 and 2. Have a reporter from each group summarize the group's ideas. Then answer question 3 as a class. Students may wish to copy the list generated to have models of language for future use.

Application: In creating conversations for this activity, students may want to refer to the Tips and the language they learned in Lesson 10 as well as ideas from this lesson. Have teams perform their conversations. As a class, evaluate each solution and the process by which the team reached that solution.

Lesson 13: Giving and Getting Feedback

Workers are continually evaluated on the job, formally and informally. They may also be expected to evaluate the work of their peers. Students must be prepared to understand, respond to, and give informal feedback. They need to learn why and how formal written evaluations are used, and they must be able to distinguish between constructive and negative criticism.

Warm-Up (page 84)

Experience: Make sure students understand the terms *evaluate* and *evaluation.* Refer to the picture in Key Words. Use examples such as tests and grades (formal evaluations) and comments from teachers or classmates (informal evaluations) to clarify. Ask students how they are evaluated at work, and elicit ideas about why they get evaluated. Ask if they think evaluations can help or harm them and why. Let them know that your work is evaluated, and so is everyone's in one way or another. For example, discuss ways in which the work of even the president of the United States is evaluated and by whom (e.g., by Congress, by voters, by the press).

Picture: Elicit predictions about who the men are, what their relationship is, and how they might be feeling. Have students identify reasons for their responses (dress, body language, expression, etc.).

Conversation and Tips (page 85)

Read the title and introduction together. Ask students for ideas of other things that are as important as hard work. Discuss the term *feedback,* and compare it to *evaluation.* Review the Tips, and tell students to listen for how they are used in the conversation.

Listen to the tape. Discuss any idioms students do not understand, and note that they will be reviewed later in the lesson. Ask if students know people like Barry, and if so, what it is like to work with them. Discuss the tone in which the two men speak. Ask students to describe the emotions Barry expresses, and record the terms they use.

Check Your Understanding (page 86)

Discuss the Questions: Ask if students think Rick followed the Tips or not, and why they think that. Trace the use of the Tips in the conversation. After students respond to question 4, have them develop a set of tips for getting feedback.

Understanding Idioms (page 87)

Refer to Barry's use of idioms in the conversation. If necessary, model the exercise by reading item 1, then finding the sentence in the conversation. Ask students to explain what the idiom means or guess from the context and to find the matching explanation on page 87. After students complete the exercise, elicit other situations in which each idiom could be used.

Extension: Have students listen to conversations of native English speakers at work, in stores, on TV, etc., and bring in other examples of idioms.

Tell them to be prepared to describe the situations in which they heard the idioms so that other students can try to guess their meaning.

Offering Advice (page 87)

Complete the exercise as a class or in small groups. For each item, have students explain why they think one choice is better than the other. Have them discuss differences in the way one talks to a friend, a co-worker, or a supervisor.

Extension: Have students create conversations between the advice-giver and the friend or role-play their interaction. The friend can be concerned, defensive, or appreciative, or have some other reaction. Have students evaluate suggestions for helping the friend solve the problem.

Try It Out (page 88)

Make sure students understand the terms *job evaluation, job review,* and *performance evaluation.* Review the directions, and have students read the performance evaluation form. Ask questions to check understanding.

To prepare for creating conversations, ask how Barry probably feels after this evaluation and what emotions he may want to express. Discuss the ways he did or did not follow Rick's advice in the conversation on page 85. Then discuss why it is useful to ask questions about a job evaluation.

Wrap-Up (page 89)

Culture: Review the directions. Have students generate interview questions to elicit the necessary information. Ask volunteers to use the example responses to model an interview.

After students conduct their interviews and complete their charts, discuss the results. Have students group the results to identify which types of feedback people are most and least interested in.

Application: Seeing a variety of evaluation forms will let students focus on common language, items evaluated, and formats. If students can't provide samples, bring in samples yourself, if possible, or refer them to the form on page 88. Then have students do the brainstorming task and create their own form. Encourage them to discuss ways to use the feedback on the sample forms and their own.

Unit 3 Review (page 90)

Review the differences between formal and informal language and when each should be used. If necessary, model the exercise by doing the first item. Then let pairs complete the remaining items. Review answers as a class, and discuss which sentence in each pair would be appropriate with co-workers, supervisors, clients, and workplace visitors.

Unit 4

Lesson 14: Following Schedules

It is critical that students understand that they must report to work on time and follow schedules in the American workplace. Students must learn how to follow work schedules, how to negotiate changes in schedules, and how overtime work is handled.

Warm-Up (page 92)

Experience: Discuss your teaching schedule. Ask what would happen if you didn't arrive on time regularly. Ask students about their own work schedules and about how work schedules in this country compare with those in their native countries. Discuss what *on time* means in the U.S. in various circumstances. Elicit the meanings of *on time* for social activities and work in students' native countries.

Conversation and Tips (page 93)

After students listen to the conversation, discuss how Diego convinces the new employee, Nasir, that the company is serious about following schedules. Ask if students know of similar policies or experiences. Discuss how Weber Corporation compensates workers for needing to follow schedules strictly. Have students talk about similar policies at their own jobs and how they could apply the Tips there.

Check Your Understanding (page 94)

Discuss the Questions: Ask if students think it is easy or difficult to get a schedule change at Weber. Elicit comparisons to their own jobs or to other workplaces.

Understanding Schedules (page 95)

Review scanning and chart-reading skills. Remind students that *scanning* here means reading quickly for specific information. Read the directions and chart title together. Have them explain the column titles (days of the week) and the row titles (shift times). Make sure they understand what the capital letters in the chart stand for (work teams). Ask a few questions to check comprehension (e.g.,

"Which teams are working from nine a.m. to five p.m. on Tuesday? How many teams are working from six a.m. to four p.m. on Thursday?"). Have students do the exercise individually or in pairs. Then review the answers, and have students re-solve any differences in their responses.

Try It Out (page 96)

Review the Master Schedule: This activity requires students to examine the relationship between work schedules and other demands or desires (e.g., child or elder care, education, recreation, hobbies). It lets them talk about the relative weight these things have in their lives.

A Difficult Decision: This activity can generate useful discussions about issues of family vs. work. It also lets students practice negotiating with a supervisor and politely turning down overtime, if necessary, while making clear that they want to work overtime in the future. After students finish role-playing, ask them to identify what strategies were most effective.

Wrap-Up (page 97)

Culture: Read or have a student read each reason aloud, but have students pick their answers individually. Discuss the responses, and have students explain their decisions. Then record the reasons that students added, and have the class discuss why those reasons are good. Have students discuss how different supervisors might react if a worker asked often for schedule changes and how schedule changes can affect the workplace.

Application: Have students compile a master list of problems and solutions. Then turn the list into a class booklet of tips.

Extension: Have students write letters and responses based on their problem/solution list in the style of an advice column.

Lesson 15: Understanding Announcements

Company bulletin boards are often communication centers. Students need to understand the function of bulletin boards and recognize the kinds of information available there. This includes standard or permanent information (e.g., OSHA rules) and time-sensitive notices (e.g., job postings, training information, announcements of upcoming events, notices of temporary changes in procedures). They should also understand which company bulletin boards allow personal announcements.

Warm-Up (page 98)

Experience: Ask if students have seen bulletin board postings at supermarkets, post offices, or schools. Elicit a list of the kinds of items posted in those places. Then discuss what kinds of items are found on bulletin boards at work. Compile a class list, and discuss why those items are important.

Picture: Have students guess what information is on the bulletin board. (After they finish the reading on page 99, you can go back and compare what they found with their guesses here.)

Reading and Tips (page 99)

Have students scan the notices quickly to identify what they're about. Give them about one minute. Then have them close the book or turn it face down. Ask them to name the subjects of as many notices as they can remember. Elicit ideas about why it can be helpful to scan a crowded bulletin board.

If necessary, teach or review common abbreviations. Ask students which topics from the notices they would like to know more about. Have them read those notices closely and summarize them for the class. Stress that most people read only the notices they consider useful. Then have students reread all the notices carefully. Discuss the Tips, and elicit ideas about how students can apply them.

Extension: Bring in or have students copy and bring in a variety of postings. Let students examine and discuss them, then compare them with items in the reading. Encourage them to bring in notices that interest them, that they don't understand, or that contain unfamiliar abbreviations.

Check Your Understanding (page 100)

Review the Information: Have students work in pairs or small groups. Have one student read an item in the exercise while the others scan the reading on page 99 for the letter of the relevant notice.

Have them rotate roles until they complete the activity. Students should be prepared to explain their choices.

Understanding Abbreviations (page 101)

After students complete the activity and review their answers, elicit examples of other abbreviations. Have them refer to the postings they brought in for the Extension activity for page 99. Discuss why bulletin board notices often contain abbreviations.

Looking at Announcements (page 101)

Read the directions together, and discuss why it might be important to distinguish between company and personal announcements. Have students work individually, compare answers, and explain their choices.

Try It Out (page 102)

Some students may already use direct deposit. If so, let them talk about why they chose it. Have students read the notice silently. Elicit explanations of any new words. Have students complete the activity individually or in pairs. Encourage them to scan the notice to quickly find the information called for. Discuss whether those who don't have direct deposit think it would be a good choice. If possible, bring in sample authorization forms to discuss.

Wrap-Up (page 103)

Culture: Make sure students understand *reimbursement*. Talk about other costs a company might reimburse. Ask students about other ways in which companies provide training.

Application: Remind students of the Warm-Up discussion of bulletin boards in public places. If possible, take the class to a post office or supermarket to look at the announcements there. After students have completed both individual and class charts, review their findings, and have them vote on the most interesting location and pick the announcements that are most interesting, most useful, and/or funniest. If any students found job postings, relate those to the topic of Lesson 16.

Lesson Extension

Have students write their own notices to post. The notices could be for services they could perform or want or for items they want to buy or sell. Encourage them to use appropriate abbreviations. Post the notices in the class for other students to read and discuss.

Lesson 16: Job Postings

Students need to understand that using the job notices posted at workplaces and employment offices can help them find new jobs, at their current workplace or elsewhere. Students also need to know how to get more information about job postings and how to decide whether or not to respond to one.

Warm-Up (page 104)

Experience: Discuss and record the various ways students have gotten jobs. If any of them used job postings, have them explain how they learned of the postings. Ask if any students have seen job notices at their workplaces, and if so, where the notices were and what jobs were available.

Picture: Discuss who the people in the picture might be and what they are looking at.

Conversation and Tips (page 105)

Read the title and introduction, and ask students what they think Hakim will talk about with Berta. Review the Tips, and make sure students understand the terms *skills, qualifications,* and *requirements*. Tell students to pay attention to how Hakim uses or doesn't use the Tips.

After students listen to the tape, discuss why Hakim was looking at the bulletin board and why he was talking to Berta. Discuss whether he is clear about his skills and his goals and how he decides whether to apply for a job. Identify ways in which he used the Tips.

Check Your Understanding (page 106)

Review the Information: Students should be prepared to use details in the conversation to explain their answers.

Discuss the Questions: After discussing question 1, ask students why companies often want workers to tell friends and relatives about available jobs and to encourage them to apply. Relate responses to question 4 to the Warm-Up discussion of how students got their jobs. Note that employment counselors urge job seekers to tell anyone they know that they are looking for a job.

Understanding a Job Posting (page 107)

Review scanning skills. Remind students that *scanning* here means reading quickly for specific information. Review the directions together. Then have students read the questions so they know what to scan for.

After students complete the activity, ask if this sounds like a good job. Discuss what factors make a job good (e.g., interesting work, good hours, good salary, chance to move up). Note that they will talk more about this posting in the next activity.

Extension: Give students copies of newspaper job ads. If they wish, they can create a job-posting bulletin board in class. (Use chart paper if a bulletin board is not available.) Have students find jobs that interest them and then apply the first Tip, determining whether their skills and qualifications meet the job requirements. Have them copy key points from the listing, using the questions on page 107 as a guide, and check points where they meet the requirements.

Try It Out (page 108)

Review the Job Posting: Explain that students should ask questions to help them decide if they want to apply for a job or not. Brainstorm some issues they should try to learn about.

Interview Questions: Ask students why it can be helpful to write possible interview questions. Help them see that they can better prepare for an interview if they anticipate questions and practice answering them.

Role-Play a Job Interview: During this exercise, the "interviewers" will use questions that the "applicants" have not seen. Discuss the importance of thinking on one's feet in an interview. After the class completes one set of interviews and evaluations, have students switch partners and do another set. Make sure students have a chance to play both roles.

After the second set of interviews, have students compare questions, comfort level, and ability of applicants to think on their feet. Discuss whether doing the first set of interviews made the second ones harder or easier. Elicit ideas about how to prepare for job interviews.

Extension: If students need to practice job interviewing, repeat this activity with other job descriptions. Use descriptions from the Extension activity on page 29, or have students bring in job notices that they are interested in.

Wrap-Up (page 109)

Culture: Have individuals share their lists with the class. If students get ideas about other skills they have, they can add those skills to their own lists. Discuss how students can use these lists when they prepare resumes.

Application: In compiling the class chart, refer back to the list created in the Warm-Up. Have students look up and record the addresses and phone numbers of state or local employment agencies.

Lesson 17: Reading Memos

Even the smallest companies rely on written or electronic communication with workers—it's efficient, and all recipients get the same information. Workers at all levels must be able to read memos and announcements to find key information, understand level of importance, and figure out how to respond. Students need to develop skills and strategies that let them do these things.

Warm-Up (page 110)

Experience: Bring in or have students bring in samples of written workplace information: letters, memos, e-mail messages, instructions, etc. Have students examine, discuss, and compare these samples. Elicit differences between memos and other forms of written communication (e.g., formatted differently, usually more concise than letters, usually phrased more formally than e-mail). Make sure students understand the term *benefits,* or introduce the concept. Discuss what employees may

earn besides their salaries. (If students don't receive employee benefits in their jobs, you can ask what benefits they know about when you move to the Word List.)

Word List: In the center of the board or a large sheet of paper, write *Job Benefits* and circle it. Elicit related items by looking at the Key Words and asking for other examples. Record or have students record any suggestions in a semantic web (grouping related ideas and using circles and lines to show connections). Then organize the suggestions into categories, and work with students to create a new web or a chart of benefits. Students can copy this version and expand it throughout the lesson.

Reading and Tips (page 111)

Have students read the memo one time quickly. Then review the Tips. Ask them what tip they've already used and what they should do next. Have them read the memo carefully a second time or listen to it on tape. Review the memo format, and discuss where specific details appear. Make sure students understand the use and meaning of *Re:* to introduce the subject line. Then have them try out the rest of the Tips. For example, ask them to check in the margin any parts they think are important. Elicit and discuss any questions about meaning or content. Ask what a new employee at UPM would have to do in response to this memo. Ask students to describe how they learned about benefits at their jobs.

Check Your Understanding (page 112)

Finding Details: After doing items 4 and 5, ask why different workers receive different numbers of vacation and sick days. After doing item 6, ask why a company would have this policy.

Understanding Written Information (page 113)

Can You? Review or explain *can* and *can't.* Use the example to model the activity. After students complete the exercise, have them use details from the reading to explain their answers.

What Benefit? Let students complete this exercise individually. Then review it as a class. If responses differ, discuss appropriate use of benefits (e.g., sick days must not be used for recreation).

Try It Out (page 114)

Have students read question 1 first. Then have them scan the memo. Ask the topic of the meeting and the answers to question 1. Make sure they understand that *FMLA* means *Family and Medical Leave Act,* and point out the way the initials are introduced in the subject line. Then have them reread the memo carefully and discuss the other questions. Ask if any students are familiar with the Family and Medical Leave Act. Bring in a copy of the law (available from the human resources department at your program or at a local library) or a simplified version for students to read and discuss.

Wrap-Up (page 115)

Culture: This exercise allows students to learn more about a job benefit and decide what they think of it.

Application: Students may wish to bring in memos from places other than work (e.g., their school, their children's schools, a landlord or neighborhood association) for this activity. Encourage them to share their memos. Have them work together, using the Tips, to read the memos and identify any necessary responses.

Lesson 18: Taking Telephone Messages

Telephone communication can be intimidating for new language learners. But courteous phone interactions and accurate message taking are crucial skills on any job. This is true whether or not the workers speak to anyone outside the company by phone. Students need to develop culturally acceptable phone skills and effective strategies for recording messages accurately. They also need to be able to use typical message formats.

Warm-Up (page 116)

Experience: Most people take messages at home or work. Have students discuss how they convey those messages. Ask what parts of message taking they find difficult and how they deal with those difficulties.

Picture: Elicit descriptions of what's happening in the picture. Ask whether students have ever ordered things by phone. If so, elicit and record

questions they had to answers, and ask about any difficulties they had.

Conversation and Tips (page 117)

Read the title and introduction together. Make sure students understand that they will hear two different conversations between Suzanna Carlsen, who is trying to place an order, and two different operators at the same company. Ask students to guess why Suzanna has to make two calls. Play the tape through once. Then play and discuss each conversation separately. Have students compare their initial guesses with what they heard in the conversations. Ask which operator students would prefer to talk to, and why. Then review the Tips.

Check Your Understanding (page 118)

Use both activities on this page to elicit all the differences between the two conversations and discuss the ways in which one is more effective than the other. Ask students how the Tips can be useful in business phone calls. If necessary, ask leading questions (e.g., *"Does Operator A sound as if she cares about the customer? Do you think Ms. Sherman will call Suzanna back after the conversation with Operator B? Do you think Suzanna will place an order with this company?"*).

Extension: After students discuss question 4 in Part B and develop advice for Operator A, have them role-play an interaction between Operator A and a supervisor or Ms. Sherman.

Taking Messages (page 119)

Completing a Message Form: Bring in sample message pads for students to examine and compare. Have them create questions to elicit the information needed to fill in the message form on page 119 and then find the information in the conversations on page 117. Discuss what an appropriate short message would be.

Answering the Phone: Read the directions together. Have students complete the exercise individually. As a class or in small groups, have students review the answers and explain why Operator A's style is poor and what makes the better way more effective.

Extension: Have students read the pairs of sentences in Part B aloud to hear the differences in tone. They can use the statements in the Better Way column to create a sample phone conversation.

Try It Out (page 120)

Work with a Partner: Read the introduction together. Divide the class into two groups. One group will be callers; the other will be trainers. Each group should read and discuss the information they need to get, then plan the questions they need to ask. They may wish to brainstorm additional questions. When both groups are prepared, create caller-trainer pairs. Have each pair sit back-to-back to simulate a phone conversation as they complete the activity. Afterwards, as a class, discuss what happened during the calls.

What's the Message? Divide the class into three groups, one for each role. Have each group read its role. Then create new groups of three students, one for each role. B should use a message form. C should not hear the message that A gives to B. After A delivers the message to B, have B pass the message sheet to C, who then carries out the message. When the activity is completed, the groups should report to the class what happened.

Extension: Have small groups write new messages with instructions for action and trade with another group. The second group will perform the instructions for the class. If the actions do not match the messages, have students determine what caused the misunderstanding and how to correct it.

Wrap-Up (page 121)

Culture: Stress that there are many reasons people need to take messages. Some are for their own use (e.g., calling for information or making an appointment and taking notes to remember what was said). After the brainstorming, if students don't have ideas for categories, ask leading questions (e.g., *"What equipment do you need to be prepared to take a message? What happens if a caller wants to leave a message and you don't have any paper or anything to write with? Have you ever written a message and then had trouble reading what you wrote?"*).

Application: This activity gives students practice in listening for information and writing clear messages. When listening to recordings, students can't ask questions to verify information. Elicit ideas of how to check information if they can't write fast enough or don't understand something.

Extension: If possible, arrange with friends, stores, or offices to allow students to call and talk to someone. Have students prepare questions they will ask and then bring messages back to the class.

Unit 4 Review (page 122)

Use the activity to review key terms and idioms for communication at work. Have students respond to items 2, 4, and 7 from their own experience. They can also revise the statements in items 1, 5, and 8, using information about their own workplaces.